THE SiMPLE SCRiPTURE jOURNAL

A NOTEBOOK FOR BOYS

WRITTEN & DESIGNED BY SHALANA FRISBY

First Printing: May 2018
1 2 3 Journal It Publishing

ISBN-13: 978-1-947209-56-5
Pocketbook 6x9-in. Format Size
From the *Christian Workbooks* Series

THiS JOURNAL
BELONGS TO

MY DAILY BIBLE VERSES FOR THE WEEK OF _____ TO _____

MONDAY:

TUESDAY:

WEDNESDAY:

THURSDAY:

FRIDAY:

- -

- -

- -

- -

SATURDAY:

- -

- -

- -

- -

SUNDAY:

- -

- -

- -

- -

THIS WEEK'S PRAISES & PRAYER REQUESTS:

____

____

____

____

____

MY DAILY BIBLE VERSES FOR THE WEEK OF _____ TO _____

MONDAY:

TUESDAY:

WEDNESDAY:

THURSDAY:

FRIDAY:

SATURDAY:

SUNDAY:

THIS WEEK'S PRAISES & PRAYER REQUESTS:

MY DAILY BIBLE VERSES FOR THE WEEK OF _____ TO _____

MONDAY:

TUESDAY:

WEDNESDAY:

THURSDAY:

FRIDAY:

SATURDAY:

SUNDAY:

THIS WEEK'S PRAISES & PRAYER REQUESTS:

____

____

____

____

____

MY DAILY BIBLE VERSES FOR THE WEEK OF ____ TO ____

MONDAY:

TUESDAY:

WEDNESDAY:

THURSDAY:

FRiDAY:

SATURDAY:

SUNDAY:

THiS WEEK'S PRAiSES & PRAYER REQUESTS:

MY DAILY BIBLE VERSES FOR THE WEEK OF _____ TO _____

MONDAY:

TUESDAY:

WEDNESDAY:

THURSDAY:

FRIDAY:

SATURDAY:

SUNDAY:

THIS WEEK'S PRAISES & PRAYER REQUESTS:

MY DAILY BIBLE VERSES FOR THE WEEK OF ＿＿＿ TO ＿＿＿

MONDAY:

TUESDAY:

WEDNESDAY:

THURSDAY:

THiS WEEK'S PRAiSES & PRAYER REQUESTS:

MY DAILY BiBLE VERSES FOR THE WEEK OF ____ TO ____

MONDAY:

TUESDAY:

WEDNESDAY:

THURSDAY:

FRIDAY:

SATURDAY:

SUNDAY:

THIS WEEK'S PRAISES & PRAYER REQUESTS:

MY DAILY BIBLE VERSES FOR THE WEEK OF ____ TO ____

MONDAY:

TUESDAY:

WEDNESDAY:

THURSDAY:

FRIDAY:

SATURDAY:

SUNDAY:

THIS WEEK'S PRAISES & PRAYER REQUESTS:

MY DAILY BIBLE VERSES FOR THE WEEK OF ____ TO ____

MONDAY:

TUESDAY:

WEDNESDAY:

THURSDAY:

FRIDAY:

SATURDAY:

SUNDAY:

THIS WEEK'S PRAISES & PRAYER REQUESTS:

MY DAILY BiBLE VERSES FOR THE WEEK OF ____ TO ____

MONDAY:

TUESDAY:

WEDNESDAY:

THURSDAY:

FRIDAY:

SATURDAY:

SUNDAY:

THIS WEEK'S PRAISES & PRAYER REQUESTS:

MY DAILY BIBLE VERSES FOR THE WEEK OF _____ TO _____

MONDAY:

TUESDAY:

WEDNESDAY:

THURSDAY:

FRIDAY:

SATURDAY:

SUNDAY:

THIS WEEK'S PRAISES & PRAYER REQUESTS:

MY DAILY BIBLE VERSES FOR THE WEEK OF ____ TO ____

MONDAY:

TUESDAY:

WEDNESDAY:

THURSDAY:

FRIDAY:

SATURDAY:

SUNDAY:

THIS WEEK'S PRAISES & PRAYER REQUESTS:

MY DAILY BIBLE VERSES FOR THE WEEK OF ____ TO ____

MONDAY:

TUESDAY:

WEDNESDAY:

THURSDAY:

THIS WEEK'S PRAISES & PRAYER REQUESTS:

MY DAILY BIBLE VERSES FOR THE WEEK OF _____ TO _____

MONDAY:

TUESDAY:

WEDNESDAY:

THURSDAY:

THiS WEEK'S PRAiSES & PRAYER REQUESTS:

MY DAILY BiBLE VERSES FOR THE WEEK OF _____ TO _____

MONDAY:

TUESDAY:

WEDNESDAY:

THURSDAY:

FRIDAY:

SATURDAY:

SUNDAY:

THIS WEEK'S PRAISES & PRAYER REQUESTS:

MY DAILY BIBLE VERSES FOR THE WEEK OF ____ TO ____

MONDAY:

TUESDAY:

WEDNESDAY:

THURSDAY:

FRIDAY:

SATURDAY:

SUNDAY:

THiS WEEK'S PRAiSES & PRAYER REQUESTS:

MY DAILY BIBLE VERSES FOR THE WEEK OF _____ TO _____

MONDAY:

TUESDAY:

WEDNESDAY:

THURSDAY:

FRIDAY:

SATURDAY:

SUNDAY:

THIS WEEK'S PRAISES & PRAYER REQUESTS:

MY DAILY BIBLE VERSES FOR THE WEEK OF _____ TO _____

MONDAY:

TUESDAY:

WEDNESDAY:

THURSDAY:

THiS WEEK'S PRAiSES & PRAYER REQUESTS:

MY DAILY BIBLE VERSES FOR THE WEEK OF ____ TO ____

MONDAY:

TUESDAY:

WEDNESDAY:

THURSDAY:

FRIDAY:

- -

- -

- -

- -

SATURDAY:

- -

- -

- -

- -

SUNDAY:

- -

- -

- -

- -

THIS WEEK'S PRAISES & PRAYER REQUESTS:

MY DAILY BIBLE VERSES FOR THE WEEK OF _____ TO _____

MONDAY:

TUESDAY:

WEDNESDAY:

THURSDAY:

FRIDAY:

- -

- -

- -

- -

SATURDAY:

- -

- -

- -

- -

SUNDAY:

- -

- -

- -

- -

THiS WEEK'S PRAiSES & PRAYER REQUESTS:

____

____

____

____

____

MY DAILY BIBLE VERSES FOR THE WEEK OF _____ TO _____

MONDAY:

TUESDAY:

WEDNESDAY:

THURSDAY:

FRIDAY:

SATURDAY:

SUNDAY:

THIS WEEK'S PRAISES & PRAYER REQUESTS:

MY DAILY BIBLE VERSES FOR THE WEEK OF _____ TO _____

MONDAY:

TUESDAY:

WEDNESDAY:

THURSDAY:

FRIDAY:

SATURDAY:

SUNDAY:

THIS WEEK'S PRAISES & PRAYER REQUESTS:

MY DAiLY BiBLE VERSES FOR THE WEEK OF _____ TO _____

MONDAY:

TUESDAY:

WEDNESDAY:

THURSDAY:

FRIDAY:

- -
- -
- -
- -

SATURDAY:

- -
- -
- -
- -

SUNDAY:

- -
- -
- -
- -

THIS WEEK'S PRAISES & PRAYER REQUESTS:

MY DAILY BIBLE VERSES FOR THE WEEK OF ____ TO ____

MONDAY:

TUESDAY:

WEDNESDAY:

THURSDAY:

THIS WEEK'S PRAISES & PRAYER REQUESTS:

MY DAILY BIBLE VERSES FOR THE WEEK OF ____ TO ____

MONDAY:

TUESDAY:

WEDNESDAY:

THURSDAY:

FRIDAY:

SATURDAY:

SUNDAY:

THiS WEEK'S PRAiSES & PRAYER REQUESTS:

MY DAILY BIBLE VERSES FOR THE WEEK OF _____ TO _____

MONDAY:

TUESDAY:

WEDNESDAY:

THURSDAY:

THiS WEEK'S PRAiSES & PRAYER REQUESTS:

MY DAILY BIBLE VERSES FOR THE WEEK OF ____ TO ____

MONDAY:

TUESDAY:

WEDNESDAY:

THURSDAY:

FRIDAY:

SATURDAY:

SUNDAY:

THIS WEEK'S PRAISES & PRAYER REQUESTS:

MY DAILY BIBLE VERSES FOR THE WEEK OF _____ TO _____

MONDAY:

TUESDAY:

WEDNESDAY:

THURSDAY:

FRIDAY:

SATURDAY:

SUNDAY:

THIS WEEK'S PRAISES & PRAYER REQUESTS:

MY DAILY BIBLE VERSES FOR THE WEEK OF ____ TO ____

MONDAY:

TUESDAY:

WEDNESDAY:

THURSDAY:

FRIDAY:

SATURDAY:

SUNDAY:

THIS WEEK'S PRAISES & PRAYER REQUESTS:

MY DAILY BiBLE VERSES FOR THE WEEK OF _____ TO _____

MONDAY:

TUESDAY:

WEDNESDAY:

THURSDAY:

FRIDAY:

SATURDAY:

SUNDAY:

THIS WEEK'S PRAISES & PRAYER REQUESTS:

MY DAILY BIBLE VERSES FOR THE WEEK OF ____ TO ____

MONDAY:

TUESDAY:

WEDNESDAY:

THURSDAY:

FRIDAY:

SATURDAY:

SUNDAY:

THIS WEEK'S PRAISES & PRAYER REQUESTS:

MY DAILY BIBLE VERSES FOR THE WEEK OF _____ TO _____

MONDAY:

TUESDAY:

WEDNESDAY:

THURSDAY:

FRIDAY:

SATURDAY:

SUNDAY:

THIS WEEK'S PRAISES & PRAYER REQUESTS:

MY DAILY BIBLE VERSES FOR THE WEEK OF ____ TO ____

MONDAY:

TUESDAY:

WEDNESDAY:

THURSDAY:

THIS WEEK'S PRAISES & PRAYER REQUESTS:

MY DAILY BIBLE VERSES FOR THE WEEK OF _____ TO _____

MONDAY:

TUESDAY:

WEDNESDAY:

THURSDAY:

FRIDAY:

SATURDAY:

SUNDAY:

THIS WEEK'S PRAISES & PRAYER REQUESTS:

MY DAILY BIBLE VERSES FOR THE WEEK OF _____ TO _____

MONDAY:

TUESDAY:

WEDNESDAY:

THURSDAY:

FRIDAY:

SATURDAY:

SUNDAY:

THIS WEEK'S PRAISES & PRAYER REQUESTS:

____

____

____

____

____

____

MY DAILY BIBLE VERSES FOR THE WEEK OF _____ TO _____

MONDAY:

TUESDAY:

WEDNESDAY:

THURSDAY:

FRiDAY:

SATURDAY:

SUNDAY:

THiS WEEK'S PRAiSES & PRAYER REQUESTS:

MY DAILY BIBLE VERSES FOR THE WEEK OF ____ TO ____

MONDAY:

TUESDAY:

WEDNESDAY:

THURSDAY:

THIS WEEK'S PRAISES & PRAYER REQUESTS:

MY DAILY BIBLE VERSES FOR THE WEEK OF _____ TO _____

MONDAY:

TUESDAY:

WEDNESDAY:

THURSDAY:

FRIDAY:

SATURDAY:

SUNDAY:

THIS WEEK'S PRAISES & PRAYER REQUESTS:

MY DAILY BIBLE VERSES FOR THE WEEK OF _____ TO _____

MONDAY:

TUESDAY:

WEDNESDAY:

THURSDAY:

FRIDAY:

- -

- -

- -

- -

SATURDAY:

- -

- -

- -

- -

SUNDAY:

- -

- -

- -

- -

THIS WEEK'S PRAISES & PRAYER REQUESTS:

____

____

____

____

____

____

MY DAILY BIBLE VERSES FOR THE WEEK OF _____ TO _____

MONDAY:

TUESDAY:

WEDNESDAY:

THURSDAY:

THIS WEEK'S PRAISES & PRAYER REQUESTS:

MY DAILY BIBLE VERSES FOR THE WEEK OF _____ TO _____

MONDAY:

TUESDAY:

WEDNESDAY:

THURSDAY:

THIS WEEK'S PRAISES & PRAYER REQUESTS:

MY DAILY BIBLE VERSES FOR THE WEEK OF _____ TO _____

MONDAY:

TUESDAY:

WEDNESDAY:

THURSDAY:

FRIDAY:

SATURDAY:

SUNDAY:

THIS WEEK'S PRAISES & PRAYER REQUESTS:

MY DAILY BIBLE VERSES FOR THE WEEK OF _____ TO _____

MONDAY:

TUESDAY:

WEDNESDAY:

THURSDAY:

FRIDAY:

SATURDAY:

SUNDAY:

THIS WEEK'S PRAISES & PRAYER REQUESTS:

____

____

____

____

____

MY DAILY BiBLE VERSES FOR THE WEEK OF ____ TO ____

MONDAY:

TUESDAY:

WEDNESDAY:

THURSDAY:

FRIDAY:

- -

- -

- -

- -

SATURDAY:

- -

- -

- -

- -

SUNDAY:

- -

- -

- -

- -

THIS WEEK'S PRAISES & PRAYER REQUESTS:

____

____

____

____

____

MY DAILY BIBLE VERSES FOR THE WEEK OF ____ TO ____

MONDAY:

TUESDAY:

WEDNESDAY:

THURSDAY:

FRIDAY:

SATURDAY:

SUNDAY:

THiS WEEK'S PRAiSES & PRAYER REQUESTS:

____

____

____

____

____

MY DAILY BiBLE VERSES FOR THE WEEK OF _____ TO _____

MONDAY:

TUESDAY:

WEDNESDAY:

THURSDAY:

FRIDAY:

SATURDAY:

SUNDAY:

THIS WEEK'S PRAISES & PRAYER REQUESTS:

MY DAILY BIBLE VERSES FOR THE WEEK OF _____ TO _____

MONDAY:

TUESDAY:

WEDNESDAY:

THURSDAY:

FRIDAY:

- -
- -
- -
- -

SATURDAY:

- -
- -
- -
- -

SUNDAY:

- -
- -
- -
- -

THIS WEEK'S PRAISES & PRAYER REQUESTS:

MY DAILY BIBLE VERSES FOR THE WEEK OF ____ TO ____

MONDAY:

TUESDAY:

WEDNESDAY:

THURSDAY:

SATURDAY:

SUNDAY:

THIS WEEK'S PRAISES & PRAYER REQUESTS:

MY DAILY BIBLE VERSES FOR THE WEEK OF ____ TO ____

MONDAY:

TUESDAY:

WEDNESDAY:

THURSDAY:

FRIDAY:

. . . .

. . . .

. . . .

. . . .

SATURDAY:

. . . .

. . . .

. . . .

. . . .

SUNDAY:

. . . .

. . . .

. . . .

. . . .

THIS WEEK'S PRAISES & PRAYER REQUESTS:

____

____

____

____

____

MY DAILY BIBLE VERSES FOR THE WEEK OF ____ TO ____

MONDAY:

TUESDAY:

WEDNESDAY:

THURSDAY:

FRIDAY:

SATURDAY:

SUNDAY:

THIS WEEK'S PRAISES & PRAYER REQUESTS:

MY DAILY BiBLE VERSES FOR THE WEEK OF _____ TO _____

MONDAY:

TUESDAY:

WEDNESDAY:

THURSDAY:

FRIDAY:

SATURDAY:

SUNDAY:

THIS WEEK'S PRAISES & PRAYER REQUESTS:

MONDAY:

TUESDAY:

WEDNESDAY:

THURSDAY:

FRIDAY:

SATURDAY:

SUNDAY:

THiS WEEK'S PRAiSES & PRAYER REQUESTS: